KEYS ON HOW TO STOP OVERTHINKING:
Guides on how to eliminate negative thoughts

Richard H.Jabobs

Table of contents

Chapter 1

What is overthinking.

Has someone ever told you, "you're overthinking it"? You're not alone. Many of us are acquainted with the feeling of overthinking, even if we haven't identified it as such. Generally, "overthinking" refers to the practice of repeated, pointless pondering. Since thoughts may be focused on many different topics, research has traditionally separated between "rumination" about the past and present, and "worry" about the future.

Am I Overthinking?

Your ability to think is one of your greatest gifts as a human being. Our brains have evolved to develop sophisticated ideas that enable us to grasp information, solve issues, plan forward, and learn from our history. Thinking has allowed us to create complex societies and develop as a species over time.

However, the age-old cliché "too much of a good thing" comes to mind here. When we overthink, worry, or ruminate, we are thinking. The distinction of "over"-thinking indicates that our thinking is not taking us anywhere and is not useful to us. So if you notice that you are stuck thinking about the same issue over and over again but are not coming to any sort of "solution," you may be overthinking. Read on for some specific examples of common topics that we tend to overthink to reflect on what, exactly, you might be overthinking.

Video: 10 Signs You Might be Overthinking:
Overthinking the Past
\ So, what types of topics do we tend to overthink? As indicated previously, "rumination" is the term typically used in research to refer to a repeated and unproductive method of thinking about the past (Nolen-Hoeksema, 1991). (Nolen-Hoeksema, 1991). Regrets and resentments could fall into this category -

have you found yourself wishing you had followed a different route in life or made a different decision at a key crossroad? On another scale, maybe you keep thinking about the embarrassing thing you said on a Zoom call last week. Regardless of what it is, you may be overthinking the past in ways that are not benefiting you in the present or future.

Overthinking the Present
It is also possible to ruminate or overthink aspects of the present, such as your circumstances, relationships, personality, or identity. Do you question day in and day out if you are in the proper relationship? How many such ideas be harming the relationship? Your connection with yourself may also be molded substantially by the views you have about yourself at the moment.
Do you prefer to think of yourself favorably or do you tend to dwell on your perceived character defects and mistakes?

Overthinking the Future

Overthinking about the future typically falls under the category of "worry." You can be concerned about something in the short term, like an approaching presentation for school or work. Or you can be worried about more long-term existential issues, such as "will I ever feel content in life?" or "what if I never meet a partner?" Regardless, it is most certainly the case that your anxieties are not assisting you in any way.

All-Access Pass - Wellness PLR Content Collection

Why is Overthinking Unhelpful?

Perhaps you've been to a happy event like a birthday celebration, but instead of enjoying the music, food, and people, you were distracted by a dispute you had the day before or the laundry list of to-dos for the following. These, or some of the examples mentioned above, may feel familiar to you, and overthinking may be getting in the way of living your life.

Of course, you don't set out to overthink, obsess, or worry. But if you have read thus far, you are certainly aware of these challenges and are trying to find out how to modify the way you think. To alter any habit, we need the correct motivation - read on for some instances of why overthinking can be so destructive and why it is so beneficial to confront.

Overthinking & Decision-Making
When you are overthinking, you are likely attempting to address an issue in your life. Am I pursuing the proper career? Is this relationship right for me? How can I get a better grasp on my finances? The catch-22 here is that overthinking damages our capacity to make judgments. van Randenborgh and colleagues observed that rumination adversely affects individuals' decision-making processes, with ruminating participants finding choices more

challenging and being less confident in their decisions (2010). (2010).

Overthinking & Anxiety

Research has identified a high link between overthinking and mood (Segerstrom et al., 2000). (Segerstrom et al., 2000). In particular, future-focused worry has been associated with anxiety (McLaughlin et al., 2007). (McLaughlin et al., 2007). This appears to make logical sense - you may be acquainted with the experience of having concerned thoughts while simultaneously suffering from nervous emotions and sensations. Temporary and persistent anxiety may be unpleasant experiences, and research shows that shifting anxious thoughts might lessen anxiety (Gana et al., 2001). (Gana et al., 2001).

Overthinking & Depression

While future-focused repeated thought (concern) has been connected with anxiety, past- and present-focused repetitive thinking (rumination) has been associated with depression (Nolen-Hoeksema, 2000). (Nolen-Hoeksema, 2000). This relationship is substantial, with rumination connected to more frequent, longer, and more severe depressive episodes.

Overthinking & Sleep
You may have found yourself laying awake at night, unable to stop the "train of thoughts" flowing through your head. Overthinking and the associated feelings of worry and sadness might significantly influence your sleep (Pillai & Drake, 2015). (Pillai & Drake, 2015). Poor sleep is, in turn, related to unfavorable health effects (Luyster et al. 2012). (Luyster et al. 2012). If you feel like overthinking is harming your physical health, read on to discover why you overthink and how to stop.
If you have read thus far and have discovered that you tend to overthink, you may feel irritated with yourself. Why am I

doing something so awful for me? It is vital to note two things here.

At its base, overthinking is an innate self-protection strategy. What do you tend to overthink? The chance is that you are concentrating on actual difficulties like money, health, employment, relationships, and purpose. Feeling in charge of these many realms may give a feeling of well-being and, of course, you want the best for yourself. However, the idea here is that thinking about these areas in an unproductive manner does nothing to enhance them. We do not overthink on purpose. Thoughts are most commonly automatic and habitual, meaning that overthinking becomes a habit - we don't lay down at night and say to ourselves, "Okay, time to ruminate for the next two hours instead of going asleep." Your brain just performs what it has done in the past.

1. Relax

Not only can overthinking rev us up and make us feel nervous, but it may go the other way too - feeling worried can lead to greater anxiety, creating a vicious cycle. You may halt this cycle in its tracks by employing relaxation methods. What sorts of activities help you relax? Perhaps it's going on a stroll, taking some deep breaths, performing yoga, or watching a feel-good movie. If you sense that you are on edge, take a step back and ask yourself what you can do for yourself to relax.

2. Practice mindfulness
If you are reading this post, you may have realized that overthinking is an issue for you and are attempting to remedy that problem. However, you don't want to fall into the comedic trap of overthinking your overthinking. That's where mindfulness comes in.

Mindfulness is not a quick fix. However, frequent practice might help you become more aware of when you are overthinking. After years of experimenting with different mindfulness techniques, I still find myself overthinking but have observed that I can more quickly identify when I am doing so, and am more readily able to push the "pause" button on those chains of thoughts. Taking a step back from detrimental habits of thinking provides me the option to pick more useful patterns of thought and behavior.

3. Get some perspective
Mindfulness and comparable contemplative activities help us to stand back from our stream of thinking to better perceive where it is headed. This capacity to take a more objective look at our ideas is crucial to eliminating overthinking. When we are overthinking, we might feel engulfed by the topic we are concentrating on and be unable to gain perspective. When you find yourself in this situation, it could be good to ask

yourself, "Will this problem still be important to me in a year, five years, etc.?"

4. Try problem-focused thinking
It might be informative to ask yourself, "Are these thoughts helpful to me?" Once you have an understanding of when you are overthinking, you may take a step back and determine how you want to go ahead. You have two possibilities here.

You understand that the topic you are overthinking is not worth concentrating on, and you move your attention and energy elsewhere.
You understand the issue at the foundation of your overthinking and build a game plan to proactively fix this problem.

This alternative is articulated succinctly by the Dalai Lama, "If there is no solution to the issue then don't spend time fretting about it. If there is a solution to the issue then don't spend time thinking about it."

5. Talk it out

A popular dictum in cognitive-behavioral treatment is, that "thoughts are not facts." It is incredibly crucial to remember this because beliefs that we have about ourselves, our history, and our future might seem like facts: "I am not a nice person because I don't like myself." As you learn to identify when your thinking may not be helpful or represent reality, it might be good to speak to someone you trust. Sometimes simply receiving an outside viewpoint might help redefine how you think about an issue.

6. Go to therapy

For some persons, the aforementioned tactics might be adequate to gain control of overthinking. But if you are struggling to overcome your overthinking, or your overthinking might be contributing to the mental health issues I mentioned like anxiety or depression, it might be worth considering seeing a mental health professional who specializes in an evidence-based practice like cognitive-behavioral therapy.

7. Learn from your pets
In his book, Why Zebras Don't Get Ulcers, Robert Sapolsky emphasizes the variations in how people feel stress compared to other animals (2004). (2004). The title of the book relates to the belief that although other animals such as zebras could suffer temporary stresses like racing from a predator, they typically do not endure persistent stress like humans. This is connected to their predisposition to live in the present moment. Your dog is not brooding over when she collapsed yesterday in front of all the dogs at the dog park or wondering about whether she is doing enough with her life. Of course, I am anthropomorphizing here - but the point is that animals provide us a terrific example of living in the now and being happy for it.

Video: How to Stop Overthinking Everything

Overthinking is precisely what it says, thinking too much.

When you ponder too much, instead of acting and doing things, you are overthinking.
When you analyze, remark, and repeat the same ideas again and again, instead of acting, you are overthinking.

Merriam Webster defines this term as To think too much about something, or devoting too much effort into thinking about or analyzing something, in a manner that is more destructive than useful.

This habit inhibits you from taking action. It eats your energy, hinders your capacity to make choices, and keeps you on a cycle of thinking and thinking again and over.

This is a mental habit that wastes your time and energy and hinders you from acting, doing new things, and making progress in your life.

It's like tying oneself to a rope that is linked to a pole and traveling in circles again and again.

In this condition, there is an increased possibility of stress, anxiety, and loss of inner calm.

On the other side, when you don't overthink, you become more efficient, tranquil, and cheerful.

What Happens When You Overthink?
You simply can't stop thinking about an event, a person, something that occurred in the past, or an issue. Instead of looking for a solution, taking initiative, and being active,

you just keep thinking and cannot get it out of your mind.

At times, when something horrible occurs, you ponder about the worst outcomes, with ideas like "what if?" or "why?".

You slip now and then into negative thinking patterns.

You worry about previous errors or present difficulties and challenges, and how they could lead to poor results.

At times, you obsess over or over-analyze your day-to-day experiences and interactions with others.

You inflate every phrase, idea, and event beyond genuinely and reasonable dimensions, reading into it things that aren't there.

If this occurs frequently, you are what psychologists term a ruminator or over-thinker.

Psychologists have shown that overthinking may be harmful to performance, and lead to anxiety and sadness.

Chapter 2

What cause overthinking.

While everyone overthinks circumstances once in a while, other individuals are afflicted by a steady flood of ideas all the time. Chronic overthinkers relive conversations they had yesterday, second-guess every choice they make, and picture dreadful scenarios all day, every day.

Thinking too much about something frequently includes more than words—overthinkers conjure up catastrophic imagery, too. Their imaginations resemble a movie where they picture their automobile driving off the road or repeating traumatic situations over and over again.

See who's hiring here, and you can even refine your search by perks, business size, remote jobs, and more. Then, sign up for our newsletter and we'll bring advice on getting the job directly to you.

Thinking too much inhibits you from getting anything done. And, it wreaks havoc on your emotions.

Destructive Thought Patterns

Overthinking frequently combines two damaging cognitive patterns—ruminating and constant worrying.

Ruminating entails pondering on the past. Thoughts may contain things like:

I shouldn't have uttered those things during the meeting yesterday. Everyone must think I'm an idiot.

I should have remained at my previous job. I would be happier than I am today.

My parents didn't educate me on how to be confident. My anxieties have always kept me back.

Persistent worrying entails negative—often catastrophic—predictions. Thoughts may contain things like:

I'm going to disgrace myself tomorrow when I do that presentation. I know I'm going to forget everything I'm supposed to say.
Everyone else will be promoted before me.
I know we won't ever have enough money to retire. We'll be too unwell to work and we'll run out of money.
Like any habit, altering your damaging thinking patterns may be a task. But, with regular effort, you can educate your brain to think differently. Here are six methods to quit overthinking everything:
1. Notice When You're Stuck in Your Head
Overthinking may become such a habit that you don't even know when you're doing it. Start paying attention to the way you think so you can become aware of the issue.

When you're rehearsing events in your head over and over, or worrying about things you can't control, accept that this isn't useful. Thinking is only effective when it leads to constructive action.

Related: 10 Simple Ways You Can Stop Yourself From Overthinking

2.   Keep the Focus on Problem-Solving\sDwelling on your issues isn't helpful—but seeking solutions is. If it's something you have some control over, consider how you might avoid the situation, or push yourself to suggest five viable remedies.

If it's something you have no control over—like a natural disaster—think about the tactics you can use to deal with it. Focus on the things you can control, including your attitude and effort.

3. Challenge Your Thoughts
It's easy to get carried away with negative thinking. So, before you decide that calling in sick is going to get you fired, or that missing one deadline will lead you to

become homeless, understand that your ideas may be exaggeratedly negative.

Remember that your emotions will interfere with your capacity to look at circumstances objectively. Take a step back and look at the facts. What proof do you have that your notion is true? What proof do you have that your concept isn't true?

Related: Avoid Overthinking Decisions With These 7 Easy Tips

4. Schedule Time for Reflection

Stewing on your issues for lengthy periods isn't useful, but momentary thought may be therapeutic. Thinking about how you might approach things differently or detecting possible dangers to your strategy may help you perform better in the future.

Incorporate 20 minutes of "thinking time" into your daily agenda. During that time frame, let yourself worry, ponder, or think over anything you like.

When your time is done, go on to something else. And, when you start overthinking things outside of your allocated time, just remind yourself that you'll need to wait until your "thinking time" to handle those concerns in your mind.

5. Learn Mindfulness Skills
It's hard to relive yesterday or fret about the future when you're living in the now. Mindfulness will help you become more aware of the here and now.
Just like any other ability, mindfulness requires practice, but with time, it may lessen overthinking. There are programs, books, apps, courses, and videos available to assist you to develop mindfulness techniques.

6. Change the Channel
Telling oneself to stop thinking about something will backfire. The more you attempt to block an idea from entering your

brain, the more probable it is to keep showing up.

Change the channel in your brain by changing your activities. Exercise, engage in discussion on an entirely another issue, or work on a project that distracts you. Doing something different will put a stop to the flood of negative thoughts.

Train Your Brain

Paying attention to the way you think may help you become more conscious of your negative mental habits. With repetition, you can educate your brain to think differently. Over time, developing better habits can help you grow the mental muscle you need to become cognitively stronger.

Controlling your thoughts.

Your mind is the most powerful tool you have for the creation of good in your life, but if not used correctly, can also be the most destructive force in your life. To control your thoughts means to influence the way you live your life.

Your mind, more specifically, your thoughts, affects your perception and therefore, your interpretation of reality. (And Here's Why Your Perception Is Your Reality)

I have heard that the average person thinks around 70,000 thoughts a day. That's a lot, especially if they are unproductive, self-abusive, and just a general waste of energy.

You can let your thoughts run amok, but why would you? It is your mind, your thoughts; isn't it time to take your power back? Isn't it time to take control?

Choose to be the person who is actively, consciously thinking your thoughts. Be someone who can control your thoughts—become the master of your mind.

When you change your thoughts, you will change your feelings as well, and you will also eliminate the triggers that set off those feelings. Both of these outcomes provide you with a greater level of peace in your mind.

I currently have a few thoughts that are not of my choosing or a response from my reprogramming. I am the master of my mind, so now my mind is quite peaceful. Yours can be too!

Before you can become the master of your mind, you must recognize that you are currently at the mercy of several unwanted "squatters" living in your mind, and they are in control of your thoughts.

If you want to be the boss of them, you must know who they are and what their motivation is, and then you can take charge and evict them.

Here are four of the "squatters" in your head that create unhealthy and unproductive thoughts.

1. The Inner Critic
This is your constant abuser who is often a conglomeration of:

Other people's words—many times your parents
Thoughts you have created based on your own or other peoples' expectations
Comparing yourself to other people, including those in the media
The things you told yourself as a result of painful experiences such as betrayal and rejection. Your interpretation creates your self-doubt and self-blame, which are most

likely undeserved in cases of rejection and betrayal.

The Inner Critic is motivated by pain, low self-esteem, lack of self-acceptance, and lack of self-love.

Why else would this person abuse you? And since this person is you—why else would you abuse yourself? Why would you let anyone treat you this badly?

2. The Worrier
This person lives in the future—in the world of "what ifs."

The Worrier is motivated by fear, which is often irrational and has no basis. Occasionally, this person is motivated by fear that what happened in the past will happen again.

3. The Reactor or Troublemaker
This is the one that triggers anger, frustration, and pain. These triggers stem

from unhealed wounds of the past. Any experience that is even closely related to a past wound will set him off.

This person can be set off by words or feelings and can even be set off by sounds and smells.

The Reactor has no real motivation and has poor impulse control. He is run by past programming that no longer serves you—if it ever did.

4. The Sleep Deprived
This can be a combination of any number of different squatters including the inner planner, the rehashes, and the ruminator, along with the inner critic and the worrier.

The Sleep Depriver's motivation can be:

As a reaction to silence, which he fights against

Taking care of the business you neglected during the day

Self-doubt, low self-esteem, insecurity, and generalized anxiety

As listed above for the inner critic and worrier

How can you control these squatters?

How to Master Your Mind

You are the thinker and the observer of your thoughts. You can control your thoughts, but you must pay attention to them so you can identify "who" is running the show—this will determine which technique you will want to use.

Begin each day to pay attention to your thoughts and catch yourself when you are thinking of undesirable thoughts.

There are two ways to control your thoughts:

Technique A – Interrupt and replace them
Technique B – Eliminate them altogether

This second option is what is known as peace of mind.

The technique of interrupting and replacing is a means of reprogramming your subconscious mind. Eventually, the replacement thoughts will become the "go-to" thoughts in applicable situations.

Use Technique A with the Inner Critic and Worrier and Technique B with the Reactor and Sleep Deprived.

1. For the Inner Critic
When you catch yourself thinking something negative about yourself (calling yourself names, disrespecting yourself, or berating yourself), interrupt it.
You can yell (in your mind), "Stop! No!" or, "Enough! I'm in control now." Then, whatever your negative thought was about yourself, replace it with an opposite or counter thought or an affirmation that begins with "I am."

For example, if your thought is, "I'm such a loser," you can replace it with, "I am a Divine Creation of the Universal Spirit. I am a perfect spiritual being learning to master the human experience. I am a being of energy, light, and matter. I am magnificent, brilliant, and beautiful. I love and approve of myself just as I am."

You can also have a dialogue with yourself to discredit the 'voice' that created the thought—if you know whose voice it is:

"Just because so-and-so said I was a loser doesn't make it true. It was his or her opinion, not a statement of fact. Or maybe they were joking and I took it seriously because I'm insecure."

If you recognize that you have recurring self-critical thoughts, you can write out or pre-plan your counter thoughts or affirmation so you can be ready.

This is the first squatter you should evict, forcefully, if necessary:

They rile up the Worrier.
The names you call yourself become triggers when called those names by others, so he also maintains the presence of the Reactor.
They are often present when you try to fall asleep so he perpetuates the Sleep Deprived.
They are a bully and are verbally and emotionally abusive.
They are the destroyer of self-esteem. They convince you that you're not worthy. They're a liar! In the interest of your self-worth, get them out!
Eliminate your worst critic and you will also diminish the presence of the other three squatters.

Replace them with your new best friends who support, encourage, and enhance your life. This is a presence you want in your mind.

2. For the Worrier
Prolonged anxiety is mentally, emotionally, and physically unhealthy. It can have long-term health implications.

Fear initiates the fight or flight response, creates worry in the mind, and creates anxiety in the body. This may make it more difficult for you to control your thoughts effectively.

You should be able to recognize a "worry thought" immediately by how you feel. The physiological signs that the fight or flight response of fear has kicked in are:

Increased heart rate, blood pressure, or surge of adrenaline
Shallow breathing or breathlessness
Muscles tense
Use the above-stated method to interrupt any thought of worry and then replace it. But this time, you will replace your thoughts

of worry with thoughts of gratitude for the outcome you wish for.

If you believe in a higher power, this is the time to engage with it. Here is an example:

Instead of worrying about my loved ones traveling in bad weather, I say the following (I call it a prayer):

"Thank you great spirit for watching over __________. Thank you for watching over his/her car and keeping it safe, road-worthy, and free of maintenance issues without warning. Thank you for surrounding him/her with only safe, conscientious, and alert drivers. And thank you for keeping him/her safe, conscientious, and alert."

Smile when you think about it or say it aloud, and phrase it in the present tense. Both of these will help you feel it and possibly even start to believe it.

If you can visualize what you are praying for, the visualization will enhance the feeling so you will increase the impact in your vibrational field.

Now, take a calming breath, slowly in through your nose, and slowly out through the mouth. Take as many as you like! Do it until you feel that you're close to being in control of your thoughts.

Replacing fearful thoughts with gratitude will decrease reactionary behavior, taking the steam out of the Reactor.

For example: If your child gets lost in the mall, the typical parental reaction that follows the fearful thoughts when finding them is to yell at them.

"I told you never to leave my sight." This reaction just adds to the child's fear level from being lost in the first place.

Plus, it also teaches them that mom and/or dad will get mad when he or she makes a mistake, which may make them lie to you or not tell you things in the future.

Change those fearful thoughts when they happen:

"Thank You (your choice of Higher Power) for watching over my child and keeping him safe. Thank you for helping me find him soon."

Then, when you see your child after this thought process, your only reaction will be gratitude, and that seems like a better alternative for all people involved.

3. For the Troublemaker, Reactor or Over-Reactor
Permanently eliminating this squatter will take a bit more attention and reflection after the fact to identify and heal the causes of the triggers. But until then, you can prevent the

Reactor from getting out of control by initiating conscious breathing as soon as you recognize his presence.

The Reactor's thoughts or feelings activate the fight or flight response just like with the Worrier. The physiological signs of his presence will be the same. With a little attention, you should be able to tell the difference between anxiety, anger, frustration, or pain.

I'm sure you've heard the suggestion to count to ten when you get angry—well, you can make those ten seconds much more productive if you are breathing consciously during that time.

Conscious breathing is as simple as it sounds—just be conscious of your breathing. Pay attention to the air going in and coming out.

Breathe in through your nose:

Feel the air entering your nostrils.
Feel your lungs filling and expanding.
Focus on your belly rising.
Breathe out through your nose:

Feel your lungs emptying.
Focus on your belly falling.
Feel the air exiting your nostrils.
Do this for as long as you like. Leave the situation if you want. This gives the adrenaline time to normalize. Now, you can address the situation in a calmer.

One of the troubles this squatter causes is that it adds to the sleep depriver's issues. By evicting or at least controlling the Reactor, you will decrease reactionary behavior, which will decrease the need for the rehashing and ruminating that may keep you from falling asleep.

Master your mind and stop the Reactor from bringing stress to you and your relationships!

Most importantly, find your real motive. What's the inner drive that can help you to keep on moving? If you're not sure, join the free Fast-Track Class – Activate Your Motivation. It's a free intensive session that will help you identify your inner drive and build your unique motivation engine around it. Join the free session here.

4. For the Sleep Deprived
(They're made up of the Inner Planner, the Rehasher, and the Ruminator, along with the Inner Critic and the Worrier.)

I was plagued with a very common problem: not being able to turn off my mind at bedtime. This inability prevented me from falling asleep and thus, getting a restful and restorative night's sleep.

Here's how I mastered my mind and evicted the Sleep Depriver and all his cronies.

I started by focusing on my breathing—paying attention to the rise and fall of my belly—but that didn't keep the thoughts out for long. (Actually, I now start with checking my at-rest mouth position to keep me from clenching.)

Then I came up with a replacement strategy that eliminated uncontrolled thinking—imagining the word in while breathing in and thinking the word out when breathing out. I would (and do) elongate the word to match the length of my breath.

When I catch myself thinking, I shift back to in, out. With this technique, I am still thinking, sort of, but the wheels are no longer spinning out of control. I am in control of my mind and thoughts, and I choose quiet.

From the first time I tried this method, I started to yawn after only a few cycles and am usually asleep within ten minutes.

For really difficult nights, I add increase attention by holding my eyes in a looking-up position (closed, of course). Sometimes I try to look toward my third eye but that hurts my eyes.

If you have trouble falling asleep because you can't shut off your mind, I strongly recommend you try this technique. I still use it every night. You can start sleeping better tonight!

You can also use this technique any time you want to:

Fall back to sleep if you wake up too soon
Shut down your thinking
Calm your feelings
Simply focus on the present moment
The Bottom Line
Your mind is a tool, and like any other tool, it can be used for constructive purposes or destructive purposes.

You can allow your mind to be occupied by unwanted, undesirable, and destructive tenants, or you can choose desirable tenants like peace, gratitude, compassion, love, and joy.

Your mind can become your best friend, your biggest supporter, and someone you can count on to be there and encourage you. You can be in control of your thoughts. The choice is yours!

www.ingramcontent.com/pod-product-compliance
Lightning Source LLC
Chambersburg PA
CBHW051936150726
47999CB00006B/2243